Helen Steiner Rice

Lovingly

**Poems for
all Seasons**

BY HELEN STEINER RICE

Heart Gifts from Helen Steiner Rice
Lovingly, Helen Steiner Rice

"LOVINGLY" I dedicate . . . each thought herein expressed . . . to ALL who read this little book . . . and may their lives be blessed . . . For only warm, responsive hearts . . . and God's Guidance from Above . . . could fill these lines with meaning . . . and with HOPE and FAITH and LOVE.

Contents

MOTHER'S DAY

EVERY DAY IS A HOLIDAY TO PRAISE AND
THANK THE LORD

DAILY THOUGHTS FOR DAILY NEEDS

HE LOVES YOU!

A WORD FROM THE AUTHOR

Selected poems for the NEW YEAR . . . for EASTER and THANKSGIVING . . . and some special CHRIST-MAS CLASSICS . . . to give HOPE and JOY to living . . . And poems with loving tributes . . . or an accolade of praise . . . for occasions that we celebrate . . . because they're SPECIAL DAYS.

So in this book are loving thoughts . . . expressed in VALENTINES . . . and MEMORIAL DAY is recognized . . . with patriotic lines . . . And MOTHER'S DAY and FATHER'S DAY . . . are celebrated yearly . . . with loving little verses . . . to say that they're loved dearly.

And then as a reminder . . . that EACH and EVERY DAY . . . is a day to glorify the Lord . . . and to follow in His way . . . there is a small collection . . . of "THOUGHTS for DAILY LIVING" . . . to show us that life's happiness . . . is not in GETTING but in GIVING.

And if I've helped in any way . . . to inspire you and cheer you . . . or if these little lines of mine . . . in any way endear you . . . or draw you any closer . . . to God and one another . . . or helped you recognize the fact . . . that every man's a "brother" . . . then I'll be very grateful . . . that God looked down on me . . . and helped me write this little book . . . and to sign it LOVINGLY.

HELEN STEINER RICE

11

Foreword

This book is a work of pure love.

Every poem, every line and word has been put into place with the tender loving care that is wrapped like a ribbon of deepest affection around all the work of Helen Steiner Rice.

You will treasure this collection of heart-warming verses, especially at the holidays. This Christmas season let the lovely poetess of Cincinnati make every one of your gifts more dear, every star and candle brighter with crystalline delight. Let her recapture for you the childhood meaning of that blessed season when "the air resounds with good cheer."

On Valentine's Day let this book show you the magic of love, the miracle of eternal springtime at Easter, the glories of the American dream during Memorial Day and Thanksgiving. But don't stop there. These poems unveil the secret of making every day a holiday.

And if you are like most people who discover Helen Steiner Rice, you will start buying copies for your friends. They will buy copies for *their* friends, in a marvelous chain reaction of love that keeps our printing presses humming. The whole process reminds us of a chain letter, except that with this kind of a chain-love-letter no one is disappointed and everyone receives a delightful surprise.

We are proud to publish this book because of what it can mean to everyone it reaches—the young, the old, the people of every race and class around the world. Recently Mr. and Mrs. A. J. Huber of Upper Darby, Pennsylvania, sent a copy of Mrs. Rice's book "Climb 'Til Your Dream Comes True" to a young medical student in India. This is the letter they received in response:

Dear Mr. and Mrs. Huber,

It touched me so to receive the Inspirational verses, and as I read them, sitting in my room alone, in the middle of the night, I thought of myself in relation to what I was reading.

You all in America are experiencing a tremendous revolution; the gigantic strides of technological advance and the ensuing disruption has shaken the world at large. We, too, here in India are hit by the same tremors that rock your nation, if only in a milder way.

Youth is most impetuous, and I will turn to God in prayer one day and question His existence another. Without a mind of my own, I'll run from author to author and, becoming confused by their abstrusities and influenced by all the complex jargon, I became, in turn, Believer, Agnostic, Atheist, Communist, Socialist, Democrat. It's sad how one attempts to row as delicate a boat as the mind in a raging sea and yet, so often, unwise as we are, we can't help ourselves.

You'll see what I mean when I say I can't thank you enough for beautiful present, "CLIMB 'TIL YOUR DREAM COMES TRUE." These verses capture the heart by their simplicity. They are no great intellectual exercise but a simple form of poetry, almost childlike, which touches upon one's closely-guarded innocence and reminds us of our true selves; the "self" we constantly attempt to hide from.

> *Sudhir*
> *January, 1970*

We wonder whether the frank uncertainties of this brilliant young man symbolize the gropings of young people all over the earth in this revolutionary age. Deeply religious at heart, they alternate between doubt and hope. Open to any philosophy that comes along, they are surrounded by voices clamoring for their souls—and they are ready to listen with equally receptive ears to communism or democracy, atheism or Christianity.

What reaches them is the utter sincerity of a person like Helen Steiner Rice, who has the uncanny power of sweeping away from religion all the theological complexities and putting it into singing lines no one can resist. We find it fascinating that it is not an "intellectual exercise" but the childlike innocence and simplicity of Mrs. Rice's verses that captured Sudhir's heart.

We believe Sudhir's final comment is profound. Anyone who can touch the inmost self has the golden key that unlocks spiritual treasure. That treasure awaits you on every page of this new collection of Helen Steiner Rice's most appealing poems. We present it to you with the hope that every line will help you find your own true self and inspire you to climb higher.

THE PUBLISHERS

New Year's Day

A NEW YEAR BRINGS A NEW BEGINNING

As the New Year starts
     and the old year ends
There's no better time
     to make amends
For all the things
     we sincerely regret
And wish in our hearts
     we could somehow forget—
We all make mistakes,
     for it's human to err,
But no one need ever
     give up in despair,
For God gives us all
     a brand-new beginning,
A chance to start over
     and repent of our sinning—

And when God forgives us
      we too must forgive
And resolve to do better
      each day that we live
By constantly trying
      to be like Him more nearly
And to trust in His wisdom
      and love Him more dearly—
Assured that we're never
      out of His care
And we're always welcome
      to seek Him in prayer.

WHAT WILL YOU DO
WITH THIS YEAR THAT'S SO NEW?

As we start a new year
     untouched and unmarred,
Unblemished and flawless,
     unscratched and unscarred,
May we try to do better
     and accomplish much more
And be kinder and wiser
     than in the year gone before—
Let us wipe our slates clean
     and start over again,
For God gives this privilege
     to all sincere men
Who will humbly admit
     they have failed many ways
But are willing to try
     and improve these "new days"
By asking God's help
     in all that they do
And counting on Him
     to refresh and renew
Their courage and faith
     when things go wrong
And the way seems dark
     and the road rough and long—
WHAT WILL YOU DO
     WITH THIS YEAR THAT'S SO NEW?
The choice is yours—
     God leaves that to YOU!

TIME IS A GIFT FROM GOD

We stand once more on the threshold
      of a shining and unblemished year,
Untouched yet by TIME and FRUSTRATION,
      unclouded by FAILURE and FEAR . . .
How will we use the days of this year
      and the TIME God has placed in our hands,
Will we waste the minutes and squander the hours,
      leaving "no prints behind in time's sands" . . .
Will we vainly complain that LIFE is SO SWIFT,
      that we haven't the TIME TO DO GOOD,
Our days are too crowded, our hours are too short
      to do ALL THE GOOD THINGS we should . . .
We say we would pray if we just had the time,
      and be kind to all those in need,
But we live in a world of "PLANNED PROGRESS"
      and our national password is "SPEED" . . .
God, grant us the grace as another year starts
      to use all the hours of our days,
Not for our own selfish interests
      and our own willful, often-wrong ways . . .
But teach us to TAKE TIME FOR PRAYING
      and to find time for LISTENING TO YOU
So each day is spent well and wisely
      doing WHAT YOU MOST WANT US TO DO.

GOD, GRANT US HOPE AND FAITH AND LOVE

HOPE for a world
        grown cynically cold,
Hungry for power
        and greedy for gold . . .

FAITH to believe
        when within and without
There's a nameless fear
        in a world of doubt . . .

LOVE that is bigger
        than race or creed,
To cover the world
        and fulfill each need . . .

        God, grant these gifts
        To all troubled hearts
        As the old year ends
        And a new year starts.

LET US SEEK GOD'S GUIDANCE
THROUGH THE YEAR

As the threatening "CLOUDS OF CHAOS"
Gather in man's muddled mind
While he searches for an answer
He alone can never find,
May God turn our vision skyward
So that we can see above
The gathering clouds of darkness
And behold God's brightening love—
For today we're facing problems
Man alone can never solve,
For it takes much more than genius
To determine and resolve
The conditions that confront us
All around on every side,
Daily mounting in intensity
Like the restless, rising tide—
But we'll find new strength and wisdom
If instead of proud resistance
We humbly call upon the Lord
And seek DIVINE ASSISTANCE,
For the spirit can unravel
Many tangled, knotted threads
That defy the skill and power
Of the world's best hands and heads—
For the plans of growth and progress
Of which we all have dreamed
Cannot survive materially
Unless THE SPIRIT is redeemed—

So as another new year dawns
Let us seek the Lord in prayer
And place our future hopes and plans
Securely in God's care.

MAKE THE YEAR A STEPPING-STONE TO GROWTH

Whatever the new year has in store
Remember there's always a good reason for
Everything that comes into our life,
For even in times of struggle and strife
If we but lift our eyes above
We see "our cross" as a "gift of love" . . .
For things that cause the heart to ache
Until we feel that it must break
Become the strength by which we climb
To higher heights that are sublime . . .
So welcome every stumbling block
And every thorn and jagged rock,
For each one is a STEPPING-STONE
To a fuller life than we've ever known,
And in the radiance of God's smiles
We learn to soar above life's trials . . .
So let us accept what the new year brings,
Seeing the HAND of GOD in ALL THINGS,
And as we grow in strength and grace
The clearer we can see God's face.

HOW TO FIND HAPPINESS
THROUGH THE YEAR

Everybody, everywhere
        seeks happiness, it's true,
But finding it and keeping it
        seems difficult to do,
Difficult because we think
        that happiness is found
Only in the places where
        wealth and fame abound—
And so we go on searching
        in "palaces of pleasure"
Seeking recognition
        and monetary treasure,
Unaware that happiness
        is just a "state of mind"
Within the reach of everyone
        who takes time to be kind—
For in making OTHERS HAPPY
        we will be happy, too,
For the happiness you give away
        returns to "shine on you."

A NEW YEAR MEDITATION

What better time
      and what better season,
What greater occasion
      or more wonderful reason
To kneel down in prayer
      and lift our hands high
To the God of creation
      who made earth and sky,
Who sent us His Son
      to live here among men
And the message He brought
      is as true NOW as THEN—
So at this glad season
      when there's joy everywhere
Let us meet our Redeemer
      at THE ALTAR OF PRAYER

Asking Him humbly
     to bless all of our days
And grant us forgiveness
     for our erring ways—
And though we're unworthy,
     dear Father above,
Accept us today
     and let us dwell in Thy love
So we may grow stronger,
     upheld by Thy grace,
And with Thy assistance
     be able to face
All the temptations
     that fill every day,
And hold onto our hands
     when we stumble and stray—
And thank you, dear God,
     for the year that now ends
And for the great blessing
     of loved ones and friends.

A PRAYER FOR THE NEW YEAR

God grant us this year a wider view
So we see others' faults through the eyes of YOU—
Teach us to judge not with hasty tongue,
Neither THE ADULT . . . nor THE YOUNG,
Give us patience and grace to endure
And a stronger faith so we feel secure,
And instead of remembering, help us forget
The irritations that caused us to fret,
Freely forgiving for some offense
And finding each day a rich recompense
In offering a friendly, helping hand
And trying in all ways to understand
That ALL OF US whoever we are
Are trying to reach "an unreachable star"—
For the GREAT and SMALL . . . the GOOD and BAD,
The YOUNG and OLD . . . the SAD and GLAD
Are asking today, "IS LIFE WORTH LIVING?"
And the ANSWER is only in LOVING and GIVING—
For only LOVE can make man kind
And KINDNESS of HEART brings PEACE of MIND,
And by giving love we can start this year
To lift the clouds of HATE and FEAR.

Valentine's Day

WHAT ARE VALENTINES?

Valentines are GIFTS of LOVE
And with the help of God above
Love can change the human race
And make this world a better place—
For love dissolves all hate and fear
And makes our vision bright and clear
So we can see and rise above
Our pettiness on "wings of love."

THE LEGEND OF THE VALENTINE

The legend says ST. VALENTINE
Was in a prison cell
Thinking of his little flock
He had always loved so well
And, wanting to assure them
Of his friendship and his love,
He picked a bunch of violets
And sent them by a dove . . .

And on the violets' velvet leaves
He pierced these lines divine
That simply said, "I LOVE YOU"
And "I'M YOUR VALENTINE" . . .
So through the years that followed,
From that day unto this,
Folks still send messages of love
And seal them with a kiss . . .

Because a SAINT in prison
Reached through prison bars one day
And picked a bunch of violets
And sent them out to say
That FAITH and LOVE can triumph,
No matter where you are,
For FAITH and LOVE are GREATER
Than the strongest prison bar.

A TRIBUTE TO THE PATRON SAINT
OF LOVE

Where there is love the heart is light,
Where there is love the day is bright,
Where there is love there is a song
To help when things are going wrong,
Where there is love there is a smile
To make all things seem more worthwhile,
Where there is love there's quiet peace,
A tranquil place where turmoils cease—
Love changes darkness into light
And makes the heart take "wingless flight"—
Oh, blest are they who walk in love,
They also walk with God above—
For God is love and through love alone
Man finds the joy that the SAINTS have known.

THE MAGIC OF LOVE

LOVE is like MAGIC
And it always will be,
For love still remains
LIFE'S SWEET MYSTERY!

LOVE works in ways
That are wondrous and strange
And there's NOTHING IN LIFE
That LOVE CANNOT CHANGE!

LOVE can transform
The most commonplace
Into beauty and splendor
And sweetness and grace!

LOVE is unselfish,
Understanding and kind,
For it sees with its HEART
And not with its mind!

LOVE is the answer
That everyone seeks—
LOVE is the language
That every heart speaks—

LOVE can't be bought,
It is priceless and free,
LOVE like pure MAGIC
Is a SWEET MYSTERY!

VALENTINES ARE LINKS OF LOVE
SENT TO FRIENDS WE'RE FONDEST OF

FRIENDSHIP is a GOLDEN CHAIN,
The links are friends so dear,
And like a rare and precious jewel
It's treasured more each year . . .
It's clasped together firmly
With a love that's deep and true,
And it's rich with happy memories
And fond recollections, too . . .

Time can't destroy its beauty
For, as long as memory lives,
Years can't erase the pleasure
That the joy of friendship gives . . .
For friendship is a priceless gift
That can't be bought or sold,
But to have an understanding friend
Is worth far more than gold . . .
And the GOLDEN CHAIN of FRIENDSHIP
Is a strong and blessed tie
Binding kindred hearts together
As the years go passing by.

"THE GLORY OF THE EASTER STORY"

In the glorious Easter Story
A troubled world can find
Blessed reassurance
And enduring peace of mind . . .
For though we grow discouraged
In this world we're living in,
There is comfort just in knowing
God has triumphed over sin . . .
For our Saviour's Resurrection
Was God's way of telling men
That in Christ we are eternal
And in Him we live again . . .
And to know life is unending
And God's love is endless, too,
Makes our daily tasks and burdens
So much easier to do . . .
For the blessed Easter Story
Of Christ the living Lord,
Makes our earthly sorrow nothing
When compared with this reward.

EACH SPRING, GOD RENEWS
HIS PROMISE

Long, long ago
        in a land far away,
There came the dawn
        of the first Easter Day,
And each year we see
        that promise reborn
That God gave the world
        on that first Easter Morn . . .
For in each waking flower
        and each singing bird,
The PROMISE of Easter
        is witnessed and heard,
And Spring is God's way
        of speaking to men
And renewing the promise
        of Easter again,
For death is a season
        that man must pass through
And, just like the flowers,
        God wakens him, too . . .
So why should we grieve
        when our loved ones die,
For we'll meet them again
        in a "cloudless sky"—
For Easter is more
        than a beautiful story,
It's the promise of life
        and ETERNAL GLORY.

"THE HOPE OF THE WORLD"

An EMPTY TOMB . . .
      a STONE ROLLED AWAY
Speak of the Saviour
      who rose Easter Day . . .
But that was centuries
      and centuries ago,
And we ask today
      WAS IT REALLY SO?
Did He walk on earth
      and live and die
And return to HIS FATHER
      TO DWELL ON HIGH?
We were not there
      to hear or see,
But our hopes and dreams
      of ETERNITY
Are centered around
      THE EASTER STORY
When Christ ascended
      and rose in glory . . .
And life on earth
      has not been the same,
Regardless of what
      the skeptics claim,
For, after the Lord
      was crucified,

Even the ones who had
      scoffed and denied
Knew that something
      had taken place
That nothing could ever
      remove or erase . . .
For HOPE was born
      in the soul of man,
And FAITH to believe
      in God's MASTER PLAN
Stirred in the hearts
      to dispel doubt and fear
And that Faith has grown
      with each passing year . . .
For the HOPE of MAN
      is THE EASTER STORY,
For life is robbed
      of all meaning and glory
Unless man knows
      that he has a "goal"
And a "resting place"
      for his searching soul.

EASTER IS A TIME
OF MANY MIRACLES

Flowers sleeping 'neath the snow,
Awakening when the Spring winds blow;
Leafless trees so bare before,
Gowned in lacy green once more;
Hard, unyielding, frozen sod
Now softly carpeted by God;
Still streams melting in the Spring,
Rippling over rocks that sing;
Barren, windswept, lonely hills
Turning gold with daffodils . . .
These miracles are all around
Within our sight and touch and sound,
As true and wonderful today
As when "the stone was rolled away"
Proclaiming to all doubting men
That in God all things live again.

THE MIRACLES OF EASTER

The sleeping earth awakens,
The robins start to sing,
The flowers open wide their eyes
To tell us it is Spring,

The bleakness of the Winter
Is melted by the sun,
The tree that looked so stark and dead
Becomes a living one . . .
These MIRACLES of EASTER,
Wrought with divine perfection,
Are the blessed reassurance
Of our Saviour's Resurrection.

EASTER THOUGHTS
FOR
THESE TROUBLED TIMES

As the Easter Season
     dawns once again,
We look on a world
     of restless men—
Men who are "driven"
     by fear and greed
And caught in a web
     of tension and speed,
Driving themselves
     and the world, as well,
Into a future
     no one can foretell—
Oh, God, instead
     of vain "driven men,"
Fill man's heart
     with true "DRIVE" again,
Spurred on by FAITH
     in GOD ABOVE
To build a new world
     of "BROTHERLY LOVE."

"WHY SHOULD HE DIE
FOR SUCH AS I"

In everything both great and small
We see the Hand of God in all,
And in the miracles of Spring
When EVERYWHERE in EVERYTHING
His handiwork is all around
And every lovely sight and sound
Proclaims the GOD of earth and sky
I ask myself "JUST WHO AM I"
That God should send His only Son
That my salvation would be won
Upon a CROSS by a sinless man
To bring fulfillment to God's Plan—
For Jesus suffered, bled and died
That sinners might be sanctified,
And to grant God's children SUCH AS I
Eternal life in that HOME on HIGH.

REJOICE! REJOICE!

"Let Not Your Heart Be Troubled"—
Let not your soul be sad—
Easter is a time of joy
When all hearts should be glad,
Glad to know that Jesus Christ
Made it possible for men
To have their sins forgiven
And, like Him, to live again . . .

So at this joyous season
May the wondrous Easter Story
Renew our Faith so we may be
Partakers of "His Glory!"

ETERNAL SPRING

Easter comes with cheeks a-glowing,
        flowers bloom and streams are flowing,
And the earth in glad surprise
        opens wide its Springtime eyes . . .
All nature heeds the call of Spring
        as God awakens everything
And all that seemed so dead and still
        experiences a sudden thrill
As Springtime lays a magic hand
        across God's vast and fertile land . . .
Oh, how can anyone stand by
        and watch a sapphire, Springtime sky
Or see a fragile flower break through
        what just a day ago or two
Seemed barren ground still hard with frost,
        but in God's world no life is lost . . .
And flowers sleep beneath the ground,
        but when they hear Spring's waking sound
They push themselves through layers of clay
        to reach the sunlight of God's Day . . .
And man, like flowers, too, must sleep
        until he is called from the "darkened deep" . . .
To live in that place where angels sing
        and where there is Eternal Spring!

THE REVELATIONS OF EASTER

The waking earth at Easter
    Reminds us it is true
That nothing ever really dies
    That is not born anew—
For Nature in her Springtime Dress
    Reveals kind Mother Earth
Awakening from her Winter's Sleep
    To give "Spring's children" birth—
So trust God's all-wise wisdom
    And doubt the Father never,
For in His Heavenly Kingdom
    There is Nothing Lost Forever!

DEATH IS THE DOOR
TO LIFE EVERMORE

We live a short while on Earth below,
Reluctant to die for we do not know
Just what "dark death" is all about
And so we view it with fear and doubt,
Not certain of what is around the bend
We look on death as the final end
To all that made us a mortal being
And yet there lies just beyond our seeing
A beautiful life so full and complete
That we should leave with hurrying feet
To walk with God by sacred streams
Amid beauty and peace beyond our dreams—
For all who believe in the risen Lord
Have been assured of this reward
And death for them is just "graduation"
To a higher realm of wide elevation—
For life on Earth is a transient affair,
Just a few brief years in which to prepare
For a life that is free from pain and tears
Where time is not counted by hours or years—
For death is only the method God chose
To colonize heaven with the souls of those
Who by their apprenticeship on Earth
Proved worthy to dwell in the land of new birth—
So death is not sad . . . it's a time for elation,
A joyous transition . . . the soul's emigration
Into a place where the soul's safe and free
To live with God through eternity!

IN THE GARDEN OF GETHSEMANE

Before the dawn of Easter
There came Gethsemane . . .
Before the Resurrection
There were hours of agony . . .
For there can be no crown of stars
Without a cross to bear,
And there is no salvation
Without FAITH and LOVE and PRAYER,
And when we take our needs to God
Let us pray as did His Son
That dark night in Gethsemane—
"THY WILL, NOT MINE, BE DONE."

"THE WAY OF THE CROSS LEADS TO GOD"

He carried the cross to Calvary,
Carried its burden for you and me,
There on the cross He was crucified
And, because He suffered and bled and died,
We know that whatever "OUR CROSS" may be,
It leads to GOD and ETERNITY . . .
For who can hope for a "crown of stars"
Unless it is earned with suffering and scars,
For how could we face the living Lord
And rightfully claim His promised reward
If we have not carried our cross of care
And tasted the cup of bitter despair . . .
Let those who yearn for the pleasures of life,
And long to escape all suffering and strife,

Rush recklessly on to an "empty goal"
With never a thought of the spirit and soul . . .
But if you are searching to find the way
To life everlasting and eternal day—
With Faith in your heart take the path He trod,
For the WAY OF THE CROSS is the WAY TO GOD.

"AFTER THE WINTER...
GOD SENDS THE SPRING"

Easter is a season
Of HOPE and JOY and CHEER,
There's beauty all around us
To see and touch and hear . . .
So, no matter how downhearted
And discouraged we may be,
New Hope is born when we behold
Leaves budding on a tree . . .
Or when we see a timid flower
Push through the frozen sod
And open wide in glad surprise
Its petaled eyes to God . . .
For this is just God saying—
"Lift up your eyes to Me,
And the bleakness of your spirit,
Like the budding springtime tree,
Will lose its wintery darkness
And your heavy heart will sing"—
For GOD never sends THE WINTER
Without THE JOY OF SPRING.

THE STORY OF THE FIRE LILY

The crackling flames rise skyward
As the waving grass is burned,
But from the fire on the veld
A great truth can be learned . . .
For the green and living hillside
Becomes a funeral pyre
As all the grass across the veld
Is swallowed by the fire . . .
What yesterday was living,
Today is dead and still,
But soon a breathless miracle
Takes place upon the hill . . .
For, from the blackened ruins
There arises life anew
And scarlet lilies lift their heads
Where once the veld grass grew . . .
And so again the mystery
Of life and death is wrought,
And man can find assurance
In this soul-inspiring thought,
That from a bed of ashes
The fire lilies grew,
And from the ashes of our lives
God resurrects us, too.

EASTER REFLECTIONS

With OUR EYES we see
   the beauty of Easter
      as the earth awakens once more . . .

With OUR EARS we hear
   the birds sing sweetly
      to tell us Spring again is here . . .

With OUR HANDS we pick
   the golden daffodils
      and the fragrant hyacinths . . .

But only with OUR HEARTS
   can we feel the MIRACLE of GOD'S LOVE
      which redeems all men . . .

And only with OUR SOUL
   can we make our "pilgrimage to God"
      and inherit His Easter Gift of ETERNAL LIFE.

THE JOY OF EASTER
WAS BORN
OF GOOD FRIDAY'S SORROW

Who said the "darkness of the night"
would never turn to day,
Who said the "winter's bleakness"
would never pass away,
Who said the fog would never lift
and let the sunshine through,
Who said the skies now overcast
would nevermore be blue—
Why should we ever entertain
these thoughts so dark and grim
And let the brightness of our mind
grow cynical and dim
When we know beyond all questioning
that winter turns to spring
And on the notes of sorrow
new songs are made to sing—
For no one sheds a teardrop
or suffers loss in vain,
For God is always there to turn
our losses into gain,
And every burden born Today
and every present sorrow
Are but God's happy harbingers
of a joyous, bright Tomorrow.

THE PROMISE OF EASTER

"BECAUSE HE LIVES WE TOO SHALL LIVE"

We need these seven words above
　　　　to help us to endure
The changing world around us
　　　　that is dark and insecure,
To help us view the present
　　　　as a passing episode,
A troubled, brief encounter
　　　　on life's short and troubled road—
For in knowing life's eternal
　　　　because our Saviour died
And arose again at Easter
　　　　after He was crucified
Makes this uncertain present,
　　　　in a world of sin and strife,
Nothing but a stepping-stone
　　　　to a NEW and BETTER LIFE!

LET US PRAY
AT THIS GLORIOUS EASTER SEASON

What better time
        or more beautiful season,
What greater occasion
        or more wonderful reason
To kneel down in prayer
        and thank God above
For ETERNAL LIFE
        the GIFT of HIS LOVE—
For in sending His Son
        to be crucified
He granted man LIFE
        because His Son died—
So at this glad season
        when there's joy everywhere
Let us meet OUR REDEEMER
        at THE ALTAR of PRAYER.

AN EASTER PRAYER

God, give us eyes to see
    the beauty of the Spring,
And to behold Your majesty
    in every living thing—
And may we see in lacy leaves
    and every budding flower
The Hand that rules the universe
    with gentleness and power—
And may this Easter grandeur
    that Spring lavishly imparts
Awaken faded flowers of faith
    lying dormant in our hearts,
And give us ears to hear, dear God,
    the Springtime song of birds
With messages more meaningful
    than man's often empty words
Telling harried human beings
    who are lost in dark despair—
"Be like us and do not worry
    for God has you in His care."

Mother's Day

"MOTHER IS A WORD CALLED LOVE"

MOTHER is a word called LOVE
And all the world is mindful of
The love that's given and shown to others
Is different from THE LOVE OF MOTHERS . . .
For Mothers play the leading roles
In giving birth to little souls,
For though "small souls" are heaven-sent
And we realize they're only lent,
It takes a Mother's loving hands
And her gentle heart that understands
To mold and shape this little life
And shelter it through storm and strife . . .
No other love than MOTHER LOVE
Could do the things required of
The one to whom God gives the keeping
Of His wee lambs, awake or sleeping,
So Mothers are a "special race"
God sent to earth to take His place,
And MOTHER is a lovely name
That even SAINTS are proud to claim.

A MOTHER'S LOVE
IS A HAVEN IN THE STORMS OF LIFE

A MOTHER'S LOVE is like an island
In life's ocean vast and wide,
A peaceful, quiet shelter
From the restless, rising tide . . .

A MOTHER'S LOVE is like a fortress
And we seek protection there
When the waves of tribulation
Seem to drown us in despair . . .

A MOTHER'S LOVE'S a sanctuary
Where our souls can find sweet rest
From the struggle and the tension
Of life's fast and futile quest . . .

A MOTHER'S LOVE is like a tower
Rising far above the crowd,
And her smile is like the sunshine
Breaking through a threatening cloud . . .

A MOTHER'S LOVE is like a beacon
Burning bright with FAITH and PRAYER,
And through the changing scenes of life
We can find a HAVEN THERE . . .

For A MOTHER'S LOVE is fashioned
After God's enduring love,
It is endless and unfailing
Like the love of HIM above . . .

For God knew in HIS great wisdom
That HE couldn't be EVERYWHERE,
So HE put HIS LITTLE CHILDREN
In a LOVING MOTHER'S CARE.

WHAT IS A MOTHER?

It takes a Mother's LOVE
    to make a house a home,
A place to be remembered,
    no matter where we roam . . .
It takes a Mother's PATIENCE
    to bring a child up right,
And her COURAGE and her CHEERFULNESS
    to make a dark day bright . . .
It takes a Mother's THOUGHTFULNESS
    to mend the heart's deep "hurts,"
And her SKILL and her ENDURANCE
    to mend little socks and shirts . . .
It takes a Mother's KINDNESS
    to forgive us when we err,
To sympathize in trouble
    and bow her head in prayer . . .
It takes a Mother's WISDOM
    to recognize our needs
And to give us reassurance
    by her loving words and deeds . . .
It takes a Mother's ENDLESS FAITH,
    her CONFIDENCE and TRUST
To guide us through the pitfalls
    of selfishness and lust . . .

And that is why in all this world
　　　　there could not be another
Who could fulfill God's purpose
　　　　as completely as a MOTHER!

MOTHERS WERE ONCE DAUGHTERS

Every home should have a daughter,
　　　　for there's nothing like a girl
To keep the world around her
　　　　in one continuous whirl . . .
From the moment she arrives on earth,
　　　　and on through womanhood,
A daughter is a FEMALE
　　　　who is seldom understood . . .
One minute she is laughing,
　　　　the next she starts to cry,
Man just can't understand her
　　　　and there's just no use to try . . .
She is soft and sweet and cuddly,
　　　　but she's also wise and smart,
She's a wondrous combination
　　　　of a mind and brain and heart . . .

And even in her baby days
　　　she's just a born coquette,
And anything she really wants
　　　she manages to get . . .
For even at a tender age
　　　she uses all her wiles
And she can melt the hardest heart
　　　with the sunshine of her smiles . . .
She starts out as a rosebud
　　　with her beauty unrevealed,
Then through a happy childhood
　　　her petals are unsealed . . .
She's soon a sweet girl graduate,
　　　and then a blushing bride,
And then a lovely woman
　　　as the rosebud opens wide . . .
And some day in the future,
　　　if it be God's gracious will,
She, too, will be a Mother
　　　and know that reverent thrill
That comes to every Mother
　　　whose heart is filled with love
When she beholds the "angel"
　　　that God sent her from above . . .
And there would be no life at all
　　　in this world or the other
Without a DARLING DAUGHTER
　　　who, in turn, becomes a MOTHER!

A MOTHER'S LOVE

A Mother's love is something
        that no one can explain,
It is made of deep devotion
        and of sacrifice and pain,
It is endless and unselfish
        and enduring come what may
For nothing can destroy it
        or take that love away . . .
It is patient and forgiving
        when all others are forsaking,
And it never fails or falters
        even though the heart is breaking . . .
It believes beyond believing
        when the world around condemns,
And it glows with all the beauty
        of the rarest, brightest gems . . .
It is far beyond defining,
        it defies all explanation,
And it still remains a secret
        like the mysteries of creation . . .
A many splendored miracle
        man cannot understand
And another wondrous evidence
        of God's tender guiding hand.

"FLOWERS LEAVE THEIR FRAGRANCE ON THE HAND THAT BESTOWS THEM"

There's an old Chinese proverb
      that, if practiced each day,
Would change the whole world
      in a wonderful way—
Its truth is so simple,
      it's so easy to do,
And it works every time
      and successfully, too—
For you can't do a kindness
      without a reward,
Not in silver nor gold
      but in joy from the Lord—
You can't light a candle
      to show others the way
Without feeling the warmth
      of that bright little ray—
And you can't pluck a rose,
      all fragrant with dew,
Without part of its fragrance
      remaining with you . . .
And whose hands bestow
      more fragrant bouquets
Than Mother who daily
      speaks kind words of praise?
A Mother whose courage
      and comfort and cheer
Lights bright little candles
      in hearts through the year—

No wonder the hands
of an UNSELFISH MOTHER
Are symbols of sweetness
unlike any other.

A MOTHER'S DAY PRAYER

"OUR FATHER in HEAVEN
whose love is divine,
Thanks for the love
of a Mother like mine—
And in Thy great mercy
look down from Above
And grant this dear Mother
the GIFT of YOUR LOVE—
And all through the year,
whatever betide her,
Assure her each day
that You are beside her—
And, Father in Heaven,
show me the way
To lighten her tasks
and brighten her day,
And bless her dear heart
with the insight to see
That her love means more
than the world to me."

WHERE THERE IS LOVE

Where there is love the heart is light,
Where there is love the day is bright,
Where there is love there is a song
To help when things are going wrong . . .
Where there is love there is a smile
To make all things seem more worthwhile,
Where there is love there's quiet peace,
A tranquil place where turmoils cease . . .
Love changes darkness into light
And makes the heart take "wingless flight" . . .
And Mothers have a special way
Of filling homes with love each day,
And when the home is filled with love
You'll always find God spoken of,
And when a family "prays together,"
That family also "stays together" . . .
And once again a Mother's touch
Can mold and shape and do so much
To make this world a better place
For every color, creed and race—
For when man walks with God again,
There shall be PEACE on EARTH for MEN.

A MOTHER'S FAREWELL TO
HER CHILDREN

When I must leave you
    for a little while,
Please do not grieve
    and shed wild tears
And hug your sorrow
    to you through the years,
But start out bravely
    with a gallant smile;
And for my sake
    and in my name
Live on and do
    all things the same,
Feed not your loneliness
    on empty days,
But fill each waking hour
    in useful ways,
Reach out your hand
    in comfort and in cheer
And I in turn will comfort you
    and hold you near;
And never, never
    be afraid to die,
For I am waiting
    for you in the sky!

MOTHERS NEVER REALLY DIE—
THEY JUST KEEP HOUSE
UP IN THE SKY

Death beckoned her with outstretched hand
And whispered softly of "AN UNKNOWN LAND"—
But she was not afraid to go
For though the path she did not know,
She took DEATH'S HAND without a fear,
For He who safely brought her here
Had told her He would lead the way
Into ETERNITY'S BRIGHT DAY . . .
And so she did not go alone
Into the "VALLEY THAT'S UNKNOWN"—
She gently took DEATH BY THE HAND
And journeyed to "THE PROMISED LAND" . . .
And there, with step so light and gay,
She polishes the sun by day
And lights the stars that shine at night
And keeps the moonbeams silvery bright . . .
For MOTHERS really never die,
They just "KEEP HOUSE UP IN THE SKY" . . .
And in the HEAVENLY HOME ABOVE
They wait to "welcome" those they love.

Memorial Day

A MEMORIAL DAY PRAYER

They SERVED and FOUGHT and DIED
    so that we might be SAFE and FREE,
Grant them, O LORD, ETERNAL PEACE
    and give them "THE VICTORY!"
And in these days of unrest,
    filled with grave uncertainty
Let's not forget THE PRICE THEY PAID
    to keep OUR COUNTRY FREE . . .
And so, on this MEMORIAL DAY,
    we offer up a prayer—
May the people of ALL NATIONS
    be UNITED in THY CARE . . .
For earth's peace and man's salvation
    can come only by Thy grace
And not through bombs and missiles
    and our quest for outer space . . .

For until all men recognize
     that "THE BATTLE IS THE LORD'S"
And peace on earth cannot be won
     with strategy and swords,
We will go on vainly fighting,
     as we have in ages past,
Finding only empty victories
     and a peace that cannot last . . .
But we've grown so rich and mighty
     and so arrogantly strong,
We no longer ask in humbleness—
     "God, show us where we're wrong" . . .
We have come to trust completely
     in the power of man-made things,
Unmindful of God's mighty power
     and that HE is "KING OF KINGS" . . .
We have turned our eyes away from HIM
     to go our selfish way,
And money, power and pleasure
     are the gods we serve today . . .
And the good green earth God gave us
     to peacefully enjoy,
Through greed and fear and hatred
     we are seeking to destroy . . .
Oh, Father, up in heaven,
     stir and wake our sleeping souls,
Renew our faith and lift us up
     and give us higher goals,
And grant us heavenly guidance
     as war threatens us again
For, more than GUIDED MISSILES,
     all the world needs GUIDED MEN.

GOD BLESS AMERICA

"AMERICA THE BEAUTIFUL"—
May it always stay that way—
But to keep "OLD GLORY" flying
There's a price that we must pay . . .
For everything worth having
Demands work and sacrifice,
And FREEDOM is a GIFT from GOD
That commands the HIGHEST PRICE . . .
For all our wealth and progress
Are as worthless as can be
Without the FAITH that made us great
And kept OUR COUNTRY FREE . . .
Nor can our nation hope to live
Unto itself alone,
For the problems of our neighbors
Must today become our own . . .
And while it's hard to understand
The complexities of war,
Each one of us must realize
That we are fighting for
The principles of freedom
And the decency of man,
And as a Christian Nation
We're committed to God's Plan . . .
And as the LAND of LIBERTY
And a great God-fearing nation
We must protect our honor
And fulfill our obligation . . .

So in these times of crisis
Let us offer no resistance
In giving help to those who need
Our strength and our assistance—
And "THE STARS and STRIPES FOREVER"
Will remain a symbol of
A rich and mighty nation
Built on FAITH and TRUTH and LOVE.

TRIBUTE TO J.F.K.

His gallant soul has but taken flight
        into "the land where there is no night"
He is not dead,
        he has only gone on
Into a brighter
        and more wonderful dawn . . .
For his passion for justice
        among men of good will
No violence can silence,
        no bullet can still . . .
For his spirit lives on
        and, like the warm sun,
It will nourish the dreams
        that he had begun . . .
So this hour of sorrow
        is only God's will,
For the "good in this man
        is living here still" . . .

Forgive our transgressions
   and revive us anew
So we may draw closer
   to each other and YOU . . .
For unless "God is guard,"
   John Kennedy said,
"We're standing unguarded"
   with dreams that are dead . . .
For a nation too proud
   to kneel down and pray
Will crumble to chaos
   and descend to decay . . .
So use "WHAT HE GAVE"
   for a REDEDICATION
And make this once more
   a God-fearing nation—
A symbol of hope—and
   a standard for good
As we lead in the struggle
   for a "NEW BROTHERHOOD!"

Father's Day

FATHERS ARE WONDERFUL PEOPLE

Fathers are wonderful people
    too little understood,
And we do not sing their praises
    as often as we should . . .
For, somehow, Father seems to be
    the man who pays the bills,
While Mother binds up little hurts
    and nurses all our ills . . .
And Father struggles daily
    to live up to "HIS IMAGE"
As protector and provider
    and "hero of the scrimmage" . . .
And perhaps that is the reason
    we sometimes get the notion
That Fathers are not subject
    to the thing we call emotion,
But if you look inside Dad's heart,
    where no one else can see,
You'll find he's sentimental
    and as "soft" as he can be . . .

But he's so busy every day
　　　　in the gruelling race of life,
He leaves the sentimental stuff
　　　　to his partner and his wife . . .
But Fathers are just WONDERFUL
　　　　in a million different ways,
And they merit loving compliments
　　　　and accolades of praise,
For the only reason Dad aspires
　　　　to fortune and success
Is to make the family proud of him
　　　　and to bring them happiness . . .
And like OUR HEAVENLY FATHER,
　　　　he's a guardian and a guide,
Someone that we can count on
　　　　to be ALWAYS ON OUR SIDE.

IT'S SO NICE TO HAVE A DAD AROUND THE HOUSE

DADS are special people
No home should be without,
For every family will agree
They're "SO NICE TO HAVE ABOUT"—
They are a happy mixture
Of a "SMALL BOY" and a "MAN"
And they're very necessary
In every "FAMILY PLAN"—
Sometimes they're most demanding
And stern, and firm and tough,
But underneath they're "soft as silk"
For this is just a "BLUFF"—
But in any kind of trouble
Dad reaches out his hand,
And you can always count on him
To help and understand—
And while we do not praise Dad
As often as we should,
We love him and admire him,
And while that's understood,
It's only fair to emphasize
His importance and his worth—
For if there were no loving Dads
This would be a "LOVELESS EARTH!"

Thanksgiving

A THANKSGIVING DAY PRAYER

"Faith of our Fathers" renew us again
And make us a nation of God-fearing men
Seeking Thy guidance, Thy love and Thy will,
For we are but Pilgrims in need of Thee still—
And, gathered together on Thanksgiving Day,
May we lift up our hearts and our hands as we pray
To thank You for blessings we so little merit
And grant us Thy love and teach us to SHARE IT.

THANK GOD FOR LITTLE THINGS

Thank you, God, for little things
  that often come our way—
The things we take for granted
  but don't mention when we pray—
The unexpected courtesy,
  the thoughtful, kindly deed—
A hand reached out to help us
  in the time of sudden need—
Oh make us more aware, dear God,
  of little daily graces
That come to us with "sweet surprise"
  from never-dreamed-of places.

"ONE NATION UNDER GOD"

Thanksgiving is more
  than a day in November
That students of history
  are taught to remember,
More than a date
  that we still celebrate
With turkey and dressing
  piled high on our plate . . .
For while we still offer
  the traditional prayer,
We pray out of habit
  without being aware
That the pilgrims thanked God
  just for being alive,

For the strength that He gave them
　　　　to endure and survive
Hunger and hardship
　　　　that's unknown in the present
Where progress and plenty
　　　　have made our lives pleasant . . .
And living today
　　　　in this great and rich nation
That depends not on God
　　　　but on mechanization,
We tend to forget
　　　　that our forefathers came
To establish a country
　　　　under God's name . . .
But we feel we're so strong
　　　　we no longer need FAITH,
And it now has become
　　　　nothing more than a wraith
Of the faith that once founded
　　　　this powerful nation
In the name of the Maker
　　　　and the Lord of creation . . .
Oh, teach us, dear God,
　　　　we are all PILGRIMS still,
Subject alone
　　　　to Your guidance and will,
And show us the way
　　　　to purposeful living
So we may have reason
　　　　for daily thanksgiving—
And make us once more
　　　　a GOD-FEARING NATION
And not just a puppet
　　　　of controlled automation.

THANK YOU, GOD, FOR EVERYTHING

Thank you, God, for everything—
    the big things and the small,
For "every good gift comes from God"—
    the giver of them all—
And all too often we accept
    without any thanks or praise
The gifts God sends as blessings
    each day in many ways,
And so at this THANKSGIVING TIME
    we offer up a prayer
To thank you, God, for giving us
    a lot more than our share . . .
First, thank you for the little things
    that often come our way,
The things we take for granted
    but don't mention when we pray,
The unexpected courtesy,
    the thoughtful, kindly deed,
A hand reached out to help us
    in the time of sudden need . . .
Oh, make us more aware, dear God,
    of little daily graces
That come to us with "sweet surprise"
    from never-dreamed-of places—
Then, thank you for the "MIRACLES"
    we are much too blind to see,
And give us new awareness
    of our many gifts from Thee,

And help us to remember
    that the KEY to LIFE and LIVING
Is to make each prayer a PRAYER of THANKS
    and every day THANKSGIVING.

FILL YOUR HEART WITH THANKSGIVING

Take nothing for granted,
     for whenever you do
The "joy of enjoying"
     is lessened for you—
For we rob our own lives
     much more than we know
When we fail to respond
     or in any way show
Our thanks for the blessings
     that daily are ours . . .
The warmth of the sun,
     the fragrance of flowers,
The beauty of twilight,
     the freshness of dawn,
The coolness of dew
     on a green velvet lawn,
The kind little deeds
     so thoughtfully done,
The favors of friends
     and the love that someone
Unselfishly gives us
     in a myriad of ways,
Expecting no payment
     and no words of praise—
Oh, great is our loss
     when we no longer find
A thankful response
     to things of this kind,

For the JOY of ENJOYING
      and the FULLNESS of LIVING
Are found in the heart
      that is filled with THANKSGIVING.

GIVE THANKS FOR THE BLESSINGS GOD HAS SHOWN FOR "MAN CANNOT LIVE BY BREAD ALONE"

He lived in a palace
           on a mountain of gold
Surrounded by riches
           and wealth untold,
Priceless possessions
           and treasures of art,
But he died alone
           of a "HUNGRY HEART!"
For man cannot live
           by bread alone
No matter what
           he may have or own,
For though he reaches
           his earthly goal
He'll waste away
           with a "starving soul!"
But he who eats
           of HOLY BREAD
Will always find
           his spirit fed,
And even the poorest
           of men can afford
To feast at the table
           prepared by the Lord.

WHAT IS CHRISTMAS?

Is it just a day
    at the end of the year?
A gay holiday filled
    with merry good cheer?
A season for presents—
    both taking and giving?
A time to indulge
    in the pleasures of living?
Are we lost in a meaningless,
    much-huddled daze
That covers our minds
    like a gray autumn haze?
Have we closed our hearts
    to God and His love?
And turned our eyes
    from "THE BRIGHT STAR ABOVE"?
Oh, Father in heaven,
    renew and restore
The real, true meaning
    of Christmas once more,
So we can feel
    in our hearts again
That "PEACE ON EARTH,
    GOOD WILL TO MEN"

Is still a promise
     that man can claim
If "HE BUT SEEKS IT
     IN THY NAME."

WAS IT REALLY SO?

A Star in the sky, an Angel's voice
Telling the world—REJOICE! REJOICE!
But that was centuries and centuries ago,
And we ask today, WAS IT REALLY SO?
Was the Christ Child born in a manger bed
Without a pillow to rest His head?
Did He walk on earth and live and die
And return to God to dwell on high?

We were not there to hear or see,
But our hopes and dreams of ETERNITY
Are centered around that holy story
When God sent us HIS SON IN GLORY—
And life on earth has not been the same,
Regardless of what the skeptics claim,
For no event ever left behind
A transformation of this kind . . .

So question and search and doubt, if you will,
But the STORY OF CHRISTMAS is living still . . .
And though man may conquer the earth and the sea,
He cannot conquer ETERNITY . . .
And with all his triumph man is but a clod
UNTIL HE COMES TO REST WITH GOD.

THE MIRACLE OF CHRISTMAS

Miracles are marvels
That defy all explanation
And "CHRISTMAS IS A MIRACLE"
And not just a "celebration"—
For when the true significance
Of this so-called Christmas Story
Penetrates the minds of men
And transforms them with its glory,
Then only can rebellious man
So hate-torn with dissension
Behold his adversaries
With a broader "new dimension"—
For we can only live in peace
When we learn to "love each other"
And accept all human beings
With the compassion of a brother—
And it takes the CHRIST of CHRISTMAS
To change man's point of view
For only through the CHRIST CHILD
Can all men be born anew,
And that is why God sent His Son
As a Christmas Gift of Love
So that wickedness and hatred,
Which the world had so much of,
Could find another outlet
By following in Christ's way
And discovering a new power
That violence can't outweigh—
And in the CHRISTMAS STORY
Of the HOLY CHRIST CHILD'S BIRTH
Is THE ANSWER to a BETTER WORLD
And GOOD WILL and PEACE on EARTH.

IF THERE HAD NEVER BEEN
A CHRISTMAS

If God had never sent His Son
To dwell with man on earth,
If there had been no Christmas
To herald the Christ Child's birth,
If in this world of violence
And hatred, crime and war
There were absolutely nothing
That made life worth living for,
If whenever man was troubled
And lost in loneliness,
There were no haven for his heart
To calm his restlessness,
Then life would be intolerable
And loathsome with disgust,
For there would be no love at all,
Just ugliness and lust—
And there would be no EASTER
And no resurrected Lord,
No promise of ETERNITY
And no heavenly reward—
So let us thank OUR FATHER
That He sent HIS ONLY SON
So after this life's ended
And our work on earth is done
There's the promise of ETERNITY
Where our "cross" becomes a "crown"
When all our trials are over
And we lay our burden down.

"GOD SO LOVED THE WORLD"

Our Father Up In Heaven,
      long, long years ago,
Looked down in His great mercy
      upon the earth below
And saw that folks were lonely
      and lost in deep despair
And so He said, "I'll send My Son
      to walk among them there . . .
So they can hear Him speaking
      and feel His nearness, too,
And see the many miracles
      that Faith alone can do . . .
For if man really sees Him
      and can touch His healing hand
I know it will be easier
      to Believe and Understand" . . .
And so The Holy Christ Child
      came down to live on earth
And that is why we celebrate
      His holy, wondrous birth,
And that is why at Christmas
      the world becomes aware
That heaven may seem far away
      but God Is Everywhere.

THE PRICELESS GIFT OF CHRISTMAS

Now Christmas is a season
   for joy and merrymaking,
A time for gifts and presents,
   for giving and for taking,
A festive, friendly, happy time
   when everyone is gay—
But have we ever really felt
   the GREATNESS of the Day? . . .
For through the centuries the world
   has wandered far away
From the beauty and the meaning
   of the HOLY CHRISTMAS DAY . . .
For Christmas is a heavenly gift
   that only God can give,
It's ours just for the asking,
   for as long as we shall live,
It can't be bought or bartered,
   it can't be won or sold,
It doesn't cost a penny,
   and it's worth far more than gold . . .

It isn't bright and gleaming
          for eager eyes to see,
It can't be wrapped in tinsel
          or placed beneath a tree,
It isn't soft and shimmering
          for reaching hands to touch,
Or some expensive luxury
          you've wanted very much . . .
For the PRICELESS GIFT OF CHRISTMAS
          is meant just for the heart
And we receive it only
          when we become a part
Of the kingdom and the glory
          which is ours to freely take,
For God sent the Holy Christ Child
          at Christmas for our sake,
So man might come to know Him
          and feel His Presence near
And see the many miracles
          performed while He was here . . .
And this PRICELESS GIFT OF CHRISTMAS
          is within the reach of all,
The rich, the poor, the young and old,
          the greatest and the small . . .
So take HIS PRICELESS GIFT OF LOVE,
          REACH OUT and YOU RECEIVE,
And the only payment that God asks
          is just that YOU BELIEVE.

IN CHRIST WHO WAS BORN AT CHRISTMAS
ALL MEN MAY LIVE AGAIN

Let us all remember
When our faith is running low,
Christ is more than just a figure
Wrapped in an ethereal glow—
For He came and dwelt among us
And He knows our every need
And He loves and understands us
And forgives each sinful deed—
He was crucified and buried
And rose again in glory
And His promise of salvation
Makes the wondrous Christmas Story
An abiding reassurance
That the little Christ Child's birth
Was the beautiful beginning
Of God's Plan for PEACE on EARTH.

THE GIFT OF GOD'S LOVE

All over the world at this season,
Expectant hands reach to receive
Gifts that are lavishly fashioned,
The finest that man can conceive . . .
For, purchased and given at Christmas
Are luxuries we long to possess,
Given as favors and tokens
To try in some way to express
That strange, indefinable feeling
Which is part of this glad time of year
When streets are crowded with shoppers
And the air resounds with good cheer . . .
But back of each tinsel-tied package
Exchanged at this gift-giving season,
Unrecognized often by many,
Lies a deeper, more meaningful reason . . .
For, born in a manger at Christmas
As a gift from the Father above,
An infant whose name was called Jesus
Brought mankind the GIFT OF GOD'S LOVE . . .
And the gifts that we give have no purpose
Unless God is part of the giving,
And unless we make Christmas a pattern
To be followed in everyday living.

"A LITTLE CHILD SHALL LEAD THEM"

God sent the little Christ Child
So man might understand
"That a little child shall lead them"
To that unknown "Promised Land" . . .
For God in His great wisdom
Knew that men would rise to power
And forget His Holy Precepts
In their great triumphal hour . . .
He knew that they would question
And doubt the Holy Birth
And turn their time and talents
To the pleasures of this earth . . .
But every new discovery
Is an open avenue
To more and greater mysteries,
And man's search is never through . . .
And man can never fathom
The mysteries of the Lord
Or understand His promise
Of a heavenly reward . . .
And no one but a LITTLE CHILD
With simple FAITH and LOVE
Can lead man's straying footsteps
To HIGHER REALMS ABOVE.

"I AM THE LIGHT OF THE WORLD"

Oh, Father, up in heaven, we have wandered far away
From the Holy little Christ Child
who was born on Christmas Day,
And the promise of salvation
that God promised when Christ died
We have often vaguely questioned,
even doubted and denied . . .
We've forgotten why God sent us
Jesus Christ, His Only Son,
And in arrogance and ignorance
it's OUR WILL, not THINE, BE DONE . . .
Oh, forgive us our transgressions
and stir our souls within
And make us ever conscious that there is no joy in sin,
And shed THY LIGHT upon us as Christmas comes again
So we may strive for PEACE ON EARTH
and good will among men . . .
And, God, in Thy great wisdom, Thy mercy and Thy love,
Endow man with the virtue that we have so little of . . .
For unless we have HUMILITY
in ourselves and in our nation,
We are vain and selfish puppets
in a world of automation,
And with no God to follow but the false ones we create,
We become the heartless victims
of a Godless nation's fate . . .
Oh, give us ears to hear Thee and give us eyes to see,
So we may once more seek Thee in TRUE HUMILITY.

WE'VE COME A LONG WAY
SINCE THAT FIRST CHRISTMAS DAY

We've come a long way
      since that first Christmas Night
When led by a STAR
      so wondrously bright
The Wise Men journeyed
      to find the place
That cradled the CHRIST CHILD'S
      beautiful face—
But like "lost sheep"
      we have wandered away
From God and His Son
      who was born Christmas Day,
And instead of depending
      on God's guiding hand
Ingenious man has assumed
      full command
Like the "Prodigal Son"
      who seeks to be free
From the heavenly FATHER
      and His holy decree—
But life without God
      is corroding man's soul,
Weakening his spirit
      and distorting his goal,
And unless we return
      to OUR FATHER again
We will never have PEACE
      and GOOD WILL among men—

And the freedom man sought
       will make him a slave
For only through God
       is man strong, free and brave,
So let us return
       to OUR FATHER and pray
That CHRIST is reborn
       in our hearts Christmas Day.

WHERE CAN WE FIND HIM?

Where can we find THE HOLY ONE?
Where can we see HIS ONLY SON?
The Wise Men asked, and we're asking still,
WHERE CAN WE FIND THIS MAN OF GOOD WILL?
Is He far away in some distant place,
Ruling unseen from His throne of grace?
Is there nothing on earth that man can see
To give him proof of ETERNITY?
It's true we have never looked on His face,
But His likeness shines forth from every place,
In everything both great and small
We see THE HAND OF GOD IN ALL,
And every day, somewhere, someplace,
We see THE LIKENESS OF HIS FACE . . .
For who can watch a new day's birth
Or touch the warm, life-giving earth,
Or feel the softness of the breeze
Or look at skies through lacy trees
And say they've never seen His face
Or looked upon His throne of grace . . .
And man's search for God will end and begin
When he opens his heart to let Christ in.

LET US LIVE CHRISTMAS
EVERY DAY

Christmas is more than a day
　　　　at the end of the year,
More than a season
　　　　of joy and good cheer,
Christmas is really
　　　　God's pattern for living
To be followed all year
　　　　by unselfish giving . . .
For the holiday season
　　　　awakens good cheer
And draws us closer
　　　　to those we hold dear,
And we open our hearts
　　　　and find it is good
To live among men
　　　　as WE ALWAYS SHOULD . . .

But as soon as the tinsel
        is stripped from the tree
The spirit of Christmas
        fades silently
Into the background
        of daily routine
And is lost in the whirl
        of life's busy scene,
And all unawares
        we miss and forego
The greatest blessing
        that mankind can know . . .
For if we lived Christmas
        each day, as we should,
And made it our aim
        to always do good,
We'd find the lost key
        to meaningful living
That comes not from GETTING,
        but from UNSELFISH GIVING . . .
And we'd know the great joy
        of PEACE UPON EARTH
Which was the real purpose
        of our Saviour's birth,
For in the GLAD TIDINGS
        of the first Christmas Night,
God showed us THE WAY
        AND THE TRUTH AND THE LIGHT!

A CHRISTMAS PRAYER

"O, GOD, OUR HELP IN AGES PAST,
OUR HOPE IN YEARS TO BE"—
Look down upon this PRESENT
And see our need of Thee . . .
For in this age of unrest,
With danger all around,
We need Thy hand to lead us
To higher, safer ground . . .
We need Thy help and counsel
To make us more aware
That our safety and security
Lie solely in Thy care . . .
And so we pray this Christmas
To feel THY PRESENCE near
And for Thy all-wise guidance
Throughout the coming year . . .
First, give us understanding
Enough to make us kind,
So we may judge all people
With our heart and not our mind,
Then give us strength and courage
To be honorable and true
And place our trust implicitly
In "UNSEEN THINGS" and "YOU" . . .
And help us when we falter
And renew our faith each day
And forgive our human errors
And hear us when we pray,
And keep us gently humble
In the GREATNESS OF THY LOVE
So some day we are fit to dwell
With Thee in PEACE ABOVE.

Every Day Is a Holiday to Thank and Praise the Lord

Special poems for special seasons
      are meaningful indeed,
But DAILY INSPIRATION
      is still man's greatest need—
For day by day all through the year,
      not just on holidays,
Man should glorify the Lord
      in deeds and words of praise—
And when the heart is heavy
      and everything goes wrong,
May these "Daily Words for Daily Needs"
      be like a cheery song
Assuring you "HE LOVES YOU"
      and that "YOU NEVER WALK ALONE"—
For in God's all-wise wisdom
      your EVERY NEED IS KNOWN!

Daily Thoughts for Daily Needs

If we put our problems in God's hand,
There is nothing we need understand—
It is enough to just believe
That what we need we will receive.

Life is a mixture of sunshine and rain,
Teardrops and laughter, pleasure and pain—
We can't have all bright days, but it's certainly true
There was never a cloud that
The Sun Didn't Shine Through!

The more you love, the more you'll find
That life is good and friends are kind . . .
For only What We Give Away
Enriches Us from Day to Day.

Often we stand at life's crossroads
And view what we think is the end,
But God has a much bigger vision
And HE tells us it's "ONLY A BEND."

Everything is by comparison,
Both the BITTER and the SWEET,
And it takes a bit of both of them
To make our life complete.

Oh, make us more aware, dear God,
Of little daily graces
That come to us with "sweet surprise"
From never-dreamed-of places!

You can't pluck a rose all fragrant with dew
Without part of the fragrance
remaining on you!

God never sends the WINTER
without the JOY of SPRING . . .
And though today your heart may "cry"—
tomorrow it will "SING!"

He Loves You!

It's amazing and incredible,
But it's as true as it can be,
God loves and understands us all
And that means YOU and ME—
His grace is all sufficient
For both the YOUNG and OLD,
For the lonely and the timid,
For the brash and for the bold—
His love knows no exceptions,
So never feel excluded,
No matter WHO or WHAT you are
Your name has been included—
And no matter what your past has been,
Trust God to understand,
And no matter what your problem is
Just place it in His Hand—
For in all of our UNLOVELINESS
This GREAT GOD LOVES US STILL,
He loved us since the world began
And what's more, HE ALWAYS WILL!

Easter - April 22, 1984

To my wife
the girl that I
married, the woman
I love, the mother
who shares, the
person who cares.

All my love
Ken